Saint-Malo, Brittany, France

The History, World War II, Pirates, Present Value and Tourism

Author
Leon Shaw.

Publisher:
SONITTEC LTD
College House, 2nd
Floor
17 King Edwards
Road,
Ruislip
London
HA4 7AE

Table of Content

Summary

Why Travel and Tourism Is More Important
Now Than Ever
I believe that travel expands our minds, broadens
our perspectives, and teaches us tolerance to
cultures and mentalities that are different from
our own. More importantly, travel opens our
hearts and makes us more humane and
compassionate towards others.

When we travel especially across borders we see
that people are fundamentally the same, despite
differences in culture, religion or belief. No
matter what happens between countries and
governments, people are people. We are all

searching for the same things: a better life, a better future for their children and more purpose.

Finding Positivity and Hope

Amidst all the negativity surrounding the world these days, we need to find more positivity and hope in our lives. And travel lets you do just that. Travel spreads love and shows us the goodness in people.

I've lost count of the number of encounters I've had with people who have touched my heart. Because of this, the importance of travel to me has always been incredibly clear.

Like that time when I lost my wallet in Tirana, Albania and a young man helped me out by lending me some money and making sure I got home safely.

Or the other time when I couldn't find my way out of the maze-like old town of Yadz in Iran, and a middle-aged man kindly gave me a free lift and even invited me to have tea with his wife in their home. And another time when I fell sick while biking around Bagan, Myanmar, and a kind lady who was selling drinks on the streets ushered me straight into her stall and nursed me for hours.

Albania, Iran and Myanmar are all places that many consider "dangerous", and yet the people I met there are some of the kindest souls. What we read on the news are just that the news while individual stories are what we really need to hear, and yet they remain untold.

I cannot stress how different the stories on the ground can be to what we see on TV or in the newspapers. I recently traveled to Brussels and Istanbul just a few months after the terrorist attacks. And as I expected, everything actually had returned to normal, besides the few additional security measures. Once again, it goes to show that reality is different from what the media feeds us. So get out there and see for yourself. The world really isn't such a scary place.

The importance of travel is still great

In times of distress like these, we need travel.

We need more love and positivity in this world. We need to unite and stay together, because we are always more powerful as a unit. There's a need for us to choose good over evil. We need to believe in others and see the beauty in people and the world once again.

If we stop traveling, we stop flourishing. We stop accepting people who are different to us and we stop connecting with the world. Let's break down

borders and build bridges that connect all of us
because together, we can fight fear by traveling.

Introduction

The beautiful city of St Malo in Brittany curves out to sea on a stunning natural harbour that has created some of the best sandy beaches on the Emerald Coast.

Rising out of the granite rock, St Malo is a maze of medieval streets bursting with history and culture. The legacy of the dastardly pirates of the 19th century and the siege during the Second World War entwines with the bustling array of arty shops and the delicious smells from restaurants, outdoor markets and cafes, for a romantic atmosphere. Oysters and crêpes are local delicacies to be enjoyed throughout the restaurants and markets of the town.

Intra-Muros, the ancient walled town, forms the heart of St Malo where the stunning Gothic and Romanesque Cathédrale de St Malo dominates the skyline. Walking along its ramparts, visitors can see spectacular views of the town and harbour, including the islands and forts scattered just out at sea. The pretty islands of Grand Be and Petit Be can be visited on foot at low tide, with the Fort National reachable on foot from St Malo's longest beach, the Grand Plage. If you enjoy hiking, the GR 34 coastal path travels right around the Emeral Coast and extends across most of Brittany's coast from Mont St Michel to Le Tour-de-Parc.

Just outside of the city is the town of St Servan where the imposing Tour Solidor contains a museum dedicated to the French sailors who first negotiated Cape Horn. The Grand Aquarium is home to the Shark's Ring, an immense tank containing 3 metre long sharks, and the Nautibus submersible and is also not to be missed. Travel a little further out from the town into the surrounding countryside and you'll find the Malouinières, the mansions of the shipbuilders and corsairs who made the town rich and famous in the 18th century.

With so many crêperies in the town, you'll be sure to find somewhere to try Brittany's famous galettes, savoury pancakes made with buckwheat and filled with ham, sausage, cheese, scallops and whatever you else might choose, as well as the sweet crêpes. Thin and crispy gavottes covered in chocolate and caramel au beurre salé are also popular tasty treats. Don't forget to try some locally brewed cidre!

About St. Malo France

St Malo is about 100 miles from the D-Day beaches in Normandy. Although D-Day was on 6th June, little progress to the West was made by the Allies until the beginning of August. The 83rd Division was part of Patton's 3rd Army, and while most of the 3rd Army turned east out of the Cotentin Peninsula toward Paris, the 83rd Division turned west into Brittany through Coutances and Avranches. The coastal towns of St. Malo and Dinard being their goal.

Strategically, the battle for St. Malo is not known as a major battle but that should not take anything away from those who fought in it and their achievements. It is a story that could have come straight from the pen of a Hollywood script writer, an American commander with the improbable name of Major Speedie (329th Infantry) and a "mad" German Colonel von Aulock, complete with monacle and flapping coat. Von Aulock said he would hold out to the last man in an ancient fortress that had been heavily reinforced with concrete and contained underground tunnels, storage areas, power plants, ammo dumps, living quarters, and even a hospital, fortifications that had been built up to a level even greater than those on the Normandy beaches. Von Aulock was a veteran of Stalingrad and he was very experienced in street fighting and defense of a city fortification.

On August 6th the Germans demolished all the quays, locks, breakwaters and machinery in the harbour area in order to prevent a working harbour falling in to the hands of the approaching U.S. Army. The ancient city fortress had been heavily reinforced with concrete and and so the battle to take it was extremely difficult, and required heavy fighting to conquer these fortified German strongholds. The thick walls designed to withstand medieval siege proved effective against the modern artillery of the 83rd. The guns pummeled the city for two days. Shells from tank destroyers, 8-inch howitzers and large 155 mm guns had little or no effect. Squadrons of medium and heavy bombers produced no apparent result. Fires had become out of control, flames and thick black smoke poured from much of the city.

Colonel Von Aulock realizing that their were still many French civilians within the citys walls, arranged a cease fire to allow them to evacuate. Once the civilians fled from the town, the fighting continued. Finally, under a cover of an artillery barrage and with the limited visibility from all the smoke, the troops raced across a causeway, past the chateau, and through the gates into the town itself. Once inside the walled city, only a few enemy troops remained in the burned, ruined, and demolished buildings. However the defenders in the chateau still held out, their machine guns firing at the engineers attempting to place demolition charges against the walls. Only after concentrated artillery and tank fire, combined with the hopelessness of the situation prompted the Germans in the chateau to surrender. Just 180 of the 865 buildings within St Malo's great city walls were still standing following the surrender.

Opposite the heavily fortified city on the other side of the harbour was the Citadel itself, defended by German troops battle wise from the Normandy campaign.

Colonel Andreas Von Aulock had vowed that he would "never surrender" and "would fight to the last man" was keeping to his word. Even in his precarious position the colonel stubbornly refused to be intimidated by the Americans. He believed that a major German counterattack would relieve some of the pressure on his besieged garrison. However when the attack stalled he found that he was on his own. After a medium level bombardment of artillery fire, a coordinated attack was launched on the Citadel.

The U.S troops along with some French Resistance volunteers succeeded in getting on top of the fort, but were soon driven back by artillery fire from an Island off the coast and by machine gun and mortar fire from inside the fort.

Another attack was made and was again repelled. Not giving up the Americans fired 3-in., 105mm, 155mm, and 8-in guns at the fort, some at point blank range. Medium and heavy Bombers dropped tons of ordnance on the fort . Many 500 and 1000 pound bombs along with 100 pound incendiaries blasted the Citadel with no effect. Tank destroyers assisted by division artillery pounded the Citadel for two straight days. Two 8 inch guns of the Corps artillery came within 1500 yards of the fort and fired directly into the port holes and vents.

Von Aulock signalled Hitlers headquarters: Mein Führer, the citadel will fall today or tomorrow. All the towers have been shot away, all the guns are out of action. We will do our utmost. There was no response.

Lt. Col. Seth McKee flying a P-38 Lockheed Lightning dropped a 165 gallon tank of "Jellied Gasoline", later to become known as napalm through a ventilator on his first pass over the Citadel. In McKee's words, "On the date of the raid I was a Lt. Col. serving as Deputy Commander of the 370th Fighter Group. Our group was assigned to the Ninth Tactical Command which in turn was assigned to the 9th Air Force. We were stationed at La Vielle, Calvados, France (Site A-19) and were equipped with P-38s known as Lockheed Lightnings. I don't recall whether this was a group strength mission or just a squadron of which we had three. If group, it would have been either 36 or 48 aircraft. If it was a squadron mission it would have been either 12 or 16 aircraft. Whatever our strength, we were carrying napalm in 165 gallon belly tanks beneath our wings where we would normally carry our external fuel tanks. We were the first group to use napalm in Europe and used it often."

"I only remember this mission as, out of 69 that I flew, it was the only one where the enemy ran up the white flag during our attack. We dropped the tanks in varying fashion depending on the target and in the St. Malo case they were delivered in a dive bombing pass which we made in two aircraft elements. Being the leader, I was the first on target with my wingman. The remainder of the aircraft were in trail behind me.

The tanks were more for area targets than pinpoint targets as they were not designed to be bombs but were our normal external tanks filled with napalm in lieu of the fuel that they normally contained with phosphorus grenades attached as igniters. I guess I got lucky as my tank went down a ventilator shaft and immediately depleted all tunnels of their oxygen. When I pulled up off my target I looked back over my shoulder and observed a large white flag waving near the area of my tank's impact area. I immediately called the rest of my formation and called off the rest of the attack. At about the same time I received a call from the forward Controller requesting we call off the attack. We did so and delivered the rest of our weapons on other targets as directed

World War II
St Malo Surrenders

As the German situation in both the East and the West grew more serious Hitler was to make increasingly desperate demands upon his forces. He had always been reluctant to allow retreats. Now he was to insist that certain locations were to be turned into "fortresses", defensive citadels where his troops were expected to fight to the last man, holding up the general advance of the Allies for as long as possible. There were still plenty of fanatical Nazis prepared to follow such orders.

As the U.S. forces swept through Brittany they were to encounter a series of such fortresses established in the ports which might assist the Allies bring men and munitions straight onto the European continent. Cherbourg had not held out nearly as long as Hitler had hoped, although the port infrastructure had been so badly damaged it was of limited use to the Allies. Elsewhere the Germans held out for rather longer and the U.S. Third Army's attempts to winkle them out were to cause extensive damage to these ancient towns. However, not all of the defenders proved to be as fanatical as Hitler hoped.

'Festung St Malo' surrendered on 17th August after a fortnight of hammering by bombs, artillery and mortars. Everywhere lay destruction only 182 buildings out 865 still stood. Journalist Montague Lacey was present, covering events for the Daily Express:

[*A few minutes before four o'clock this afternoon, the German commander of the Citadel, Colonel von Auloch, the mad colonel with a monocle and a swaggering walk, led 605 men from the depths of his fortress and broke his promise to Hitler that he would never give in to the Americans. The colonel goose-stepped up to surrender, with a batman carrying his large black suitcase, and another in attendance round him flicking the dust from his uniform, and as they went by an American soldier called out: "What a corney show!"*

Colonel von Auloch is the man who wrote to the American commander attacking the Citadel to say that a German officer never surrenders, and for 15 days he sat tight 60 feet below ground in the safety of his underground shelter. By tonight the Americans would have been sitting on top of his fortress, which would have become a mass grave for all the men in it. By holding out, Colonel von Auloch has not affected the course of the war one jot. What he has done is to cause the almost complete destruction of the old town of St. Malo, and sow further seeds of hatred in the hearts of the French.

Even as I write, the townspeople gathered in the Place above are shouting and shaking their fists at the Germans from the Citadel. As the Germans pile into trucks to be taken away, the older men somehow look ashamed and stupid, but the young Germans are still grinning and arrogant. The Citadel fell dramatically just an hour before American infantrymen were ready to assault the fortress for the third time, and just as a squadron of Lightning bombers swept in to shower incendiary bombs on the place.

All last night and throughout this morning heavy guns had pounded the Citadel, a main blockhouse surrounded by about a dozen entrances from the mine-like caverns below. The Americans ate their lunch in the wrecked streets before they formed for the attack. At 2.30 p.m. a big white flag appeared on one of the pillboxes. No one took much notice, for at 3 o'clock a fighter-bomber attack was to be laid on. Soon after 3 o'clock the first Lightning swept in. It came down to 50 feet and planted a couple of incendiaries square on top of the

Citadel. More white flags were then run up there were now five flying in the breeze.

The pilot of the second bomber saw them and dived without dropping his bombs. But he opened up his guns as a sort of warning as he flew round followed by the rest of the squadron. The airmen waited long enough to see a batch of Germans come from the Citadel and a bunch of Americans walk up the hill to the front carrying a coloured identification flag.

Now there was a mad scramble to the Citadel. Word soon went round that the Germans had surrendered. Everyone raced down the hillside to see the sight. First out was Colonel von Auloch still barking orders to his officers and men who were almost tumbling over themselves to obey. Two senior officers were with him, one of them a naval commander. They were all trying to make an impressive display in front of the Americans.

Then a curious thing happened. An elderly German, a naval cook, broke ranks and ran up and embraced a young American soldier. The German was lucky not to be shot and the guards lowered their guns just in time. But no one interfered when the U.S. soldier put his arms round the German. They were father and son. The German spoke good American slang and was allowed to stay out of the ranks and act as interpreter. He had been 14 years in American, he said, and went back to Germany just before the outbreak of war.

Colonel von Auloch counted all his men as they filed out carrying their belongings. There were Poles amoung the party, some Russians and about a dozen Italians. Still shouting orders, Von Auloch was put in a jeep and driven away to Division Headquarters. He refused to talk about his surrender and so did his soldiers.

Down in the labyrinth of tunnels of the Citadel there was the usual destruction and signs of panic. Clothing and equipment were strewn all over the place. There was still plenty of food, water and ammunition and the usual heaps of empty bottles.

Colonel von Auloch's room was in the lowest and safest part of the fort. It was about eight feet by ten feet, and furnished only with two leather armchairs and a bed. It seemed to be the only room with a wash basin and running water.

On the desk stood an electric lamp and a telephone; nearby was a tray containing coffee, and two postcards which the colonel was about to write. I have one of these cards now. It shows a picture of Goering and Hitler smiling as they ride through cheering crowds. On the back is the stamp which the colonel had just stuck on a beautiful pictorial stamp of a fortress castle.

The big guns of the fort were wrecked, and all the Germans had left were machine-guns and other small arms. With the prisoners who came out of the Citadel was a little party of American soldiers who had been captured last Friday. They had crept up to the fortress at night with explosives in an attempt to wreck the ventilation system.

When all surrendered garrison had been driven away or marched away, several hundred French people gathered round shaking each other by the hand, cheering and singing their national anthem. And one day, soon perhaps, the Citadel where the mad colonel surrendered will be one of the sights the people of St. Malo will point out to visitors coming here again from England for their holidays].

St. Malo Pirates Experience

From windsurfing on the waves to sunbathing on the beach to swimming in the frigid English Channel, it's easy to get caught up in the outdoor activities the French town of Saint Malo has to offer. There's even a transatlantic race that departs from Saint Malo every four years, which sees sailors retrace the "Route du Rhum." But Saint Malo is much more than a coastal town with fresh air and scenic views. The Corsair City has sheltered scoundrels and villains for much of its history, including pirates, cod smugglers, and even Nazis.

The buildings that have survived the test of time are visible reminders of all the city has been through. They're also a sort of disguise: to the untrained viewer, it seems as if all is equally ancient. But much is new, reconstructed over the bones of ruined buildings. The visible history and hidden modernity make the city a place of contrast, full of hidden cracks to be explored by the active imagination. As writer Anthony Doerr said of his first encounter of the city, which would become the setting for his novel *All the Light We Cannot See*: "I felt as if I was walking through a city plucked from the imagination of Italo Calvino, a place that was part fairy-tale castle, part M. C. Escher drawing, part mist and ocean wind and lamplight."

The history of the walled medieval city of Saint Malo stretches back for centuries and includes political intrigue, brief declarations of independence, and plenty of seafaring. One of the earliest of its famous mariners was Jacques Cartier, who lead a voyage to North America in 1534. His three expeditions along the St. Lawrence River allowed France to lay claim to the territory that later became known as Canada. The first voyage from Saint Malo to Newfoundland took only 20 days, and Cartier took his men as far as Anticosti Island on that first trip, paving the way for later French exploration further into the interior.

But Cartier's expedition was only the start of the seafaring tradition, and by the 18th century, the walled town had a reputation for its fearsome corsairs, who pillaged non-French ships crossing the English Channel and Atlantic. The town was known by British mariners as the "Hornet's Nest," a name alluding to its treacherous coastline and fleet of well-trained sailors. One of the most infamous of these privateers was Robert Surcouf, said to have single-handedly killed 11 men in a duel.

When they weren't stealing goods or gold from cargo-laden ships from the Caribbean, the wily Malouins resorted to stealing salted codfish. The preserved fish were immensely popular across Europe, and especially in Spain. Unfortunately for France, however, Spanish consumers seemed to prefer British dry cod to the French version, perhaps because the British used Spanish salt to preserve it. The majority of Spanish merchants bought dry cod from British ships until the two countries went to war in 1739. With prices for dry cod plummeting in Britain and soaring in Spain, a few opportunistic merchants from Saint

Malo found ways to make the most of the booming market. Lead by the four Chenu brothers, merchant vessels out of Saint Malo set up renegade fishing settlements in southwestern Newfoundland. They took English cod and pretended it was French; they acquired English cod from the English Channel Islands and passed it off as French; and sometimes they changed the nationality of ships from English to French before heading into Spain to trade the fish. One official bemoaned the situation, saying, "The Bretons are the only ones who engage in this without scruple."

With such colorful characters splashed across the pages of the town's past, it's no wonder the Malouins worked hard to preserve the history of their home. But everything changed when war broke out in 1939. Saint Malo was occupied by German soldiers for four years, who didn't leave until late in the summer of 1944. Over the course of July and August 1944, extensive Allied bombing and German shelling caused the near-total destruction of the city. Wood-framed houses were swallowed by fire, and granite mansions were blown apart. Of the 865 buildings inside the city walls, 683 were destroyed, resulting in the loss of 2,000 dwellings. "Ruins had to be made safe or demolished; debris had to be cleared; recyclable building materials needed stockpiling; mines had to be removed; and temporary housing provided for the emergency workforce," writes scholar Hugh Clout.

Miraculously, the city came back together in less than a decade. Construction that began in 1955 was completed by 1960, including the rebuilding of 90 percent of the original structures with wider streets, improved sunlight penetration, and better air circulation. All the buildings were made using local granite for the exterior walls (though concrete could be used on the interior), and the roofs were made of slates from the Monts d'Arrée. The final touch was a new spire for the city's cathedral, put in place in 1971.

Despite the bombings the city endured, and despite the construction required to raise it from the ashes, Saint Malo's deep sense of history remains imbued in the very stones beneath the buildings. Even after great destruction, a city can retain the essence of its soul for all that its population and its streets have changed. As Doerr writes in *All the Light We Cannot See*: "The Goddess of History looked down to earth. Only through the hottest fires can purification be achieved."

The Burning of Saint Malo

In August 1944 the historic walled city of Saint Malo, the brightest jewel of the Emerald Coast of Brittany, France, was almost totally destroyed by fire. This should not have happened.

If the attacking U.S. forces had not believed a false report that there were thousands of Germans within the city it might have been saved. They ignored the advice of two citizens who got to their lines and insisted that there were less than 100 Germans the members of two anti-aircraft units in the city, together with hundreds of civilians who could not get out because the Germans had closed the gates.

A ring of U.S. mortars showered incendiary shells on the magnificent granite houses, which contained much fine panelling and oak staircases as well as antique furniture and porcelain;

33

zealously guarded by successive generations. Thirty thousand valuable books and manuscripts were lost in the burning of the library and the paper ashes were blown miles out to sea. Of the 865 buildings within the walls only 182 remained standing and all were damaged to some degree.

Churchill, in his *History of the Second World War*, said two armored and three infantry divisions were detached by Patton from the American assault forces in Normandy to clear the Brittany peninsula. The Germans, he said, "were pressed into their defensive perimeters of Saint Malo, Brest, Lorient and Saint Nazaire."

"Here," he added, "they could be penned and left to wither, thus saving the unnecessary losses which immediate assaults would have required."

This "leaving to wither" hardly happened at Saint Malo. Martin Blumenson in his book *Breakout and Pursuit* said few of the Americans who set out to take Saint Malo thought it would be a difficult task. But it wasn't long before the 8th Corps, and particularly the 83rd Ohio Division under General Macon, realized they had "a nasty job ahead of them."

The Germans' main defense was concentrated in five strongpoints built by the Todt Organization: to the west of the city, the La Cite fort, a vast subterranean complex carved out of a peninsula between the Rance estaury and the Bay of Saint Servan; in the Bay of Saint Malo, two fortified islands, Cezembre and the Grand Bey; and to the east, the Montaigne Saint Joseph and the La Varde fort, natural geographical features fortified with concrete, which were the first stubborn pockets of resistance encountered by the U.S. forces coming from that direction.

The garrison commander, Colonel Andreas von Aulock, a European representative of General Motors before the war, directed operations from the underground complex. The two AA sites within the city were operated by the Luftwaffe. One, on the walls of the castle at the eastern end, was commanded by Lieutenant Franz Kuster, a pre-war lawyer who subsequently became a judge in West Germany, and the other, in a little public garden facing the sea, was run by an Austrian sergeant.

To this day, a proportion of the citizens of Saint Malo believe the Germans deliberately burnt the city as an act of spite when they realized they were defeated. But all the evidence is against this.

There were many eye-witnesses to the shower of incendiaries launched by the Americans from the east, south and west of the city and the remains of a large number of these missiles were subsequently found in the ruins and identified by experts. There was no evidence of any German incendiary device having been used. In any case, it would have been illogical for Von Aulock, who certainly wasn't a fanatic, to try to burn out the city when he knew the AA units were still there. Besides, he had on the whole been attentive to the safety of the people. He had urged them on several occasions to leave the city, warning them of the horror of street fighting such as he had witnessed at Stalingrad. But a large proportion had preferred to stay because they felt they would be safer in the vast deep cellars created by Saint Malo's famed corsairs for storing their booty, than in the open country which might be transformed into a battlefield. They also feared that their houses might be looted of their valuables if left empty. Von Aulock decreed that any of his men caught looting would be shot, as would any NCO or officer who neglected his duty in this respect. Looting did take place, but the culprits were mainly civilians.

The Germans did, however, cause considerable damage in other respects. On 6 August, a minesweeper in the harbor shelled the cathedral spire which fell, causing extensive damage to the fabric. The excuse was that the spire was being used as an observation post by "terrorists." Von Aulock was furious and told Commander Breithaup, of the 12th minesweeper flotilla that the act "hardly covered the German navy with glory."

The harbor installations, including the massive lockgates, were blown up by the Germans on 7 August, and a number of vessels were scuttled there, thus ensuring that the port could not be used by the Allies.

Another German act was the rounding up of all the men between 16 and 60 in the city for internment at the Fort National, an historic fort on an islet near the castle, only accessible at low tide. This was Von Aulock's revenge for a skirmish which took place in the city on the night of 5-6 August. He was told that "terrorists" had fired on Germans. The French said it was a fight between German soldiers and mutinous sailors; there had been a marked slackening of discipline in the navy.

Unfortunately the fort was in the line of fire between the Americans coming from the east and the fortified island known as Le Grand Bey and inevitably a shell eventually fell in the midst of the several hundred hostages killing or mortally wounding 18.

The old city itself suffered from the exchange of fire between the Americans and the big guns in the underground fort. Many buildings were hit by shells as well as bombs dropped by aircraft.

However, if the damage had been restricted to shells and bombs, most of the city would have been spared. It was the concentrated attack with incendiary mortar shells which destroyed most buildings.

The Americans' belief in the presence of a large number of Germans within the city was fortified by two incidents. On 10 August, two jeeps carrying four Americans and five Frenchmen tried to enter the city by the main gate. The party was under the mistaken impression that it had been liberated. They came under a hail of machinegun fire. An American officer and two of the French were killed and the others taken prisoner.

The following day a truck carrying clothing and ammunition for the Resistance also tried to get in. The two occupants were captured and the vehicle was burnt.

These attacks were the work of the Luftwaffe men on the AA sites but the Americans watching about 500 yards away could well have thought in the confusion of the incidents that the defenders were a much larger force.

However, it is hard to understand why they were scornful of the news brought by the two French emissaries from the city. Yves Burgot and Jean Vergniaud were sent from the castle where they had been sheltering to ask for morphia for the wounded Americans and Germans. They were received coolly by an officer who asked how many Germans remained in the city. They told him there were less than a hundred but he would not accept this and the shelling and burning continued.

A truce was arranged on 13 August to allow the people to get out of the city. By this time a large part of it was either in flames or had been destroyed. The firemen could do little to prevent the spread of the fires as the Americans had severed the water main.

The Americans attacked with tanks on 14 August and, to their undoubted surprise, found the burning city almost empty.

The underground fortress continued to fight until August 17 when Von Aulock surrendered. He was subsequently accused of "the barbaric act of burning the corsairs' city," but after an examination of the ruins including the remains of incendiary shells and the questioning of witnesses, he was vindicated.

Tourism Information

Quick Guide

Once the feared base of pirates (*corsairs*), heavily fortified against Norman (or English) attack, today's Saint-Malo is one of the top tourist draws in Brittany. The star of the show is the atmospheric walled city (*intramuros*), largely destroyed in the Second World War but painstakingly reconstructed. The modern towns of Parame and Saint-Servan lie outside the walls. It is also the birth place of renowned French explorer Jacques Cartier who is famous for exploring Quebec.

By air

The closest airport to St-Malo is Dinard Bretagne Airport a seaside resort that is located just across the way. However, it only assures connections with the Anglo-Norman islands and England.

If you come from other parts of the world, you will land at the Rennes Bretagne Airport,which services French, European and American cities as well as Beijing and Montreal.

Once at the Rennes Airport, you'll have two options for connections with St-Malo :

1) Take the 57 Star bus that passes by just 300 meters away, at the Aire Libre stop [1.40€* per ticket, valid for one hour and purchased directly in the bus] to arrive at Place de la République. From there, take the bus line 7 from the Illenoo company, that will take you to Saint-Malo [2.30€

to 5.50€* depending on the length of your chosen trip].

2) In the second case, you will also need to go to Place de la République then to the gare ferroviaire that is located 1 km from the square, about 13 minutes walking, to take a train to Saint-Malo. About 20 trains per day can take you there in less than an hour. Expect to pay around 15€ per person for the trip at full price.

Alternatively, one could take a taxi to Dinard (€13), then change to Illenoo bus 16 (€2.10). For those trying to avoid the taxi ride, you can walk 2.8 km to Pleurtuit and take a bus to Saint-Malo, connecting through Dinard (€2.10 to €4.20, depending on the connections made).

By train
Saint-Malo's train station is located over a kilometer south of the *intramuros* area, but it's

an easy 20-min walk straight down Avenue Louis Martin. There are a few direct TGV services daily from Paris (Gare de Montparnasse), which take about three hours. Most travellers, however, will end up connecting in Rennes, from where there are hourly commuter services (50 min, €12) to Saint-Malo.

Trains to the West Coast, including Les Sables d'Olonne, La Rochelle and Bordeaux can be reached from Saint-Malo via interchanges at Rennes and Nantes.

By ferry

The ferry port is situated about 300 m south of the citadel walls and around half a kilometre from the main gate at Porte St-Vincent.

From the UK you can arrive from Poole and Weymouth on Condor Ferries. Leaving from Portsmouth with Brittany Ferries. From Jersey &

Guernsey you can take Condor Ferries which offers direct routes from both islands.

Brittany Ferries

Portsmouth - St-Malo : Year round service

7 crossings weekly

Journey time: 9 hours (day), 10¾ hours (overnight)

Condor Ferries

Weymouth - St-Malo : Year round service

7 crossings weekly (change at Jersey or Guernsey)

Journey time: from 6 hours 45 mins

Poole - St-Malo : May - September

7 crossings weekly

Journey time: from 5 hours 35 mins

Guernsey - St-Malo : Year round service

18 crossings weekly

Journey time: from 1 hour 45 mins

Jersey - St-Malo : Year round service

14 crossings weekly

Journey time: from 1 hour 15 mins

By bus/Car

The highway doesn't pass right by Saint-Malo because of its geographic location. Nevertheless, the city is well-serviced thanks to national and departmental roads that connect it to larger highways. About 75 km separate you from Rennes (around 1 hour by car), 404 km from Paris (around 4 hours and 23 minutes). We are happy to remind you that in Brittany there are no toll roads like in the rest of France, but 4-lane roads, separated by a midway. It is free, but the speed is limited to 110 km/h.

To park your vehicle, you'll have the choice between the parking souterrain Saint-Vincent, the parking spots inside the city, or the parking-relay from which you can take a free shuttle that takes you to the heart of the city. Here you'll find the parking prices or you can get a pré-paid card to enjoy a free hour of parking.

Coming from or going to Rennes, Illenoo buses serve Dinard and Titeniac, from where connections run. Costing €4.70 to €6.80 depending on the exact route taken, this is a slower but cheaper option than the train.

Public Transportation

The city is medium-sized. However, the bus lets you connect to différents quartiers rapidement. rather quickly. Multiple lines give you access to the beaches, while others allow you to connect to the outer areas. A transportation card costs 1.25€* and a 1-day ticket is worth 1.90€*. Here is the list of selling locations for transportation cards.

If, afterwards, you want to explore other cities in Brittany, you can take a bus from the resort.In Saint-Malo, you can also cross the sea to reach the Anglo-Norman islands or England.

To Get around

Saint-Malo has a good bus system, with the main terminals located at the train station and just outside the walls(St Vincent). Get a booklet with maps and times from any bus driver. A one and a half hour ticket costs €1.15. Unfortunately there are no bus services late in the evening.

The walled city is easily covered on foot, but you can also opt for a dinky "Tourist Train" that takes you and your wallet for a ride (€5.50).

T o See

- ➢ Ramparts >> (Remparts).
- ➢ The walled city >> (La Ville Intra-Muros)
- ➢ The Chateau

- The walled city view from the "Memorial 39-45"

- World's first tidal power station >>. The tidal power plant reportedly attracts 200,000 visitors per year. A canal lock in the west end of the dam permits the passage of 16,000 vessels between the English Channel and the Rance. The display centre is looking a bit tired and there isn't much to see from the barrage wall. Getting there is a bit tricky, bus routes C1 and C2 get you to within a kilometer walk.

To Do

- Watch the impressive tide.

- Walk (or jog) along the beach.

- Walk around the walls of the walled city(free).

- Visit the Festival des Folklores du Monde (World Folklores), which takes place at the beginning of July. There are dance and music performances from around the world. You can also dance when Celtic Breton bands play music in the main square of Parame district.

➢ Look at the many hundreds of sailing boats of all sizes and ages in the harbour/s.

To Buy

La cale aux trésors 2 passage de la grande hermine, intra-muros. website French delicatessen shop.Wineshop.

Shops in the city center usually close by 19 hrs, but most of them now (as of 2010) stay open every Sunday, including high street cloth stores, which before 2010 were not allowed to open on Sunday and now are allowed-

To Eat

Saint-Malo is a great place to sample Breton specialties.

➢ Breton Pancakes: not just the world-famous sweet crêpes, but also savoury galettes.

➢ Kouing Aman: this is a delicious Breton cake made with butter and sugar. Try to sample them piping hot, especially the ones with apple added in.

➢ Mussels (moules): fished in the place and available in any restaurants.

➢ Oysters (huitres): the best are from Cancale, a village near to Saint-Malo. In France, they are eaten raw.

The Intramuros area has what is quite possibly France's highest concentration of creperies and seafood restaurants. Most cater solely to tourists and are effectively identical.

Le Corps de Garde >>, the best view in the walled city as you are actually on the wall. This resto has galettes and crepes.

Cafe de Saint-Malo >>, just inside Grande Porte. The restaurant here is unspectacular, but what makes this the best deal in Intramuros is the window selling fresh seafood to go. For €5, you can get a dozen large oysters, pre-shelled, on ice and with a quartered lemon.

Petit Crêpier >>, Rue Ste Barbe, tel. +33-299409319. True to the name, this restaurant is small and has crepes, but their daily selection of seafood galettes is a cut above the pack. €10.

Coté brasserie >>, 8, rue des Cordiers (intra-muros), tel. 2-99568340. New proprietary. . seafoods and chips. Well separated smoking and non-smoking areas. €20-40.

Captain-Ice >>, Rue Jacques Cartier, Intra-Muros. This may well be the best ice cream place in town. Try Amour de Glace (Love of Ice cream) for something really yummy. Prices are slightly high, but you get big quantities and very high quality!

In St Malo you can eat at any time of day. In smaller towns nearby, tip: look out for the lunchtime menu ouvrière (workers' menu}; often there is little or no choice of dishes, but what you get is genuine French home cooking (love those fries!) for half the price, if that, of what you'll pay in a tourist centre like St Malo or Mont St Michel. (French lunchtime is sacred. Every French person observes it religiously.)

Crêperie le Tournesol >>, 4 rue des marins (Saint-Malo), 2-99403623. Brunch in St-Malo means only one thing: a galette washed down with a cup of local cider €3.50 no it's never too early.

Try the Crêperie Le Tournesol (16) at 4 Rue des Marins (00 33 2 99 40 36 23), with its terrace spilling out on to cobbled streets, from 11.30am Sunday. Its speciality galettes start at €7.50 and come with a huge variety of fillings, from smoked Breton sausage and egg to goats' cheese and Camembert. If you still have room, finish with something sweet a crêpe with hot chocolate sauce is €4.50.

To Drink

Brittany is not a renowned region for its wine. Otherwise, there are other specialities:

➢ Breton beer

There are two micro breweries in Saint Malo. Bosco and les brassins de saint malo. There are also several regional beers such as Coreff which can be found at La Belle Epoque bar and Britt beer which can be found at many supermarkets.

Chat Malo is a Breton beer but is not brewed in Saint Malo.

➢ Cider: There are two types of ciders in Saint Malo. Demi-sec and Brut. You are probably used to Brut. Demi-sec is sweeter and with a lower % of alcohol.

➢ Calvados: apple brandy

➢ Chouchen: mead (it's a blend with alcohol and honey; it is very sweet)

➢ Muscadet: dry white wine, perfect with local seafood; true, it doesn't come from Brittany, but is from the nearest vineyard area, Pays de la Loire

➢ Bars: Most bars are found in the old city of intramuros. If you want to venture into the less beautiful but also less touristic areas of Saint Malo here are some good bars. By the train station Bosco and the cafe de la gare are both a good bet. In Saint Servan the Café Cancalais is popular and in Parame a good wine bar is le jus d'octobre

To Get out

Visit nearby Mont Saint Michel - a monastery and town built on a tiny outcrop of rock in the sand, which is cut off from the mainland at high tide. It is one of France's major tourist destinations, and as such gets very busy in high season. Check the times of the tides before you visit!

Cross the Rance Tidal Dam (Barrage de la Rance) and see Dinard; especially in October when the town hosts its annual English Film Festival (lots of US films, too). Casino, sandy beaches, high cliffs studded with quaint, Victorian-era houses, many with conical tower tops; covered market.

Venture west beyond Dinard to the Côte d'Emeraude (Emerald Coast) to find even more luscious sandy beaches and little-known towns such as St-Lunaire and St-Cast (first French town to liberate itself from Nazis by own efforts, 1944) and the lonely, craggy, atmospheric Cap Fréhel, where in spring you can see gannets, the superb large seabird that never otherwise comes within sight of shore.

Despite past lives as a fortress and the site of a monastery, St-Malo is best known for the *corsaires* who used it as a base during the 17th and 18th centuries. During wartime, a decree from the French king sanctioned the seafaring mercenaries to intercept British ships and requisition their cargo. During peacetime, they acted as intrepid merchant marines, returning from Asia and the Americas with gold, coffee, and spices. Indeed, the sea is in the hearts of all *Malouins*, as natives of St-Malo are called— especially during the city's famous transatlantic sailing race, the *Route du Rhum*, which is held every 4 years and finishes in Guadeloupe.

Walking the ramparts and cobblestone streets, it's hard to imagine that 80 percent of St-Malo was destroyed in World War II. What you see today is thanks to a meticulous, decades-long restoration.

St-Malo encompasses the communities of St. Servan and Paramé, but most tourists head for the walled city, or *Intra-muros*. In summer, the Grande Plage du Sillon towards Paramé is dotted with sun-seekers; year-round it's sought after for its deluxe seawater spa. St. Servan's marina is adjacent to a large terminal where ferries depart for and arrive from the Channel Islands and England.

In the area

The Brittany coast is the region's main tourist attraction. To the east and west of Saint Malo, the Emerald Coast offers a succession of small resorts, with fine sandy beaches separated by lengths of rocky coastline.

At the eastern end of the Emerald Coast, about 50km from Saint Malo, is le Mont Saint Michel, a fabulous medieval city perched on a rock connected to the mainland by a causeway. One of the most visited tourist sites in France outside Paris, le Mont Saint Michel is classed as a UNESCO world heritage site.

The western end of the Emerald coast is Cap Fréhel, one of Brittany's great beauty spots. Just before Cap Fréhel is the spectacular clifftop castle of Fort la Latte, parts of which date from the 14th century. Fort la Latte is France's equivalent of Cornwall's Tintagel Castle, though much less of a ruin.

Dinard, across the estuary from Saint Malo, is one of France's classic up-market resorts, which became popular in the nineteenth century. It is very different from Dinan, a historic small town with an impressive medieval castle.The historic fortified old town of Dinan sits on a rise overlooking the valley of the Rance below, to which it is connected by a narrow winding cobbled pedestrianized street lined with old stone and half-timbered houses, including plenty of craft shops, boutiques or restaurants.

Twenty km southeast of Dinan, the chateau and park of Bourbansais are worth a visit, particularly for families. From April to September, there are guided visits of the chateau, a 16th - 17th century stately home seven days a week, mostly in the afternoon however the gardens and the zoo are open all year. The Bourbansais zoo is heavily committed in programmes for the protection and breeding of endangered species.

St-Malo Weather

St-Malo and the coast of north eastern Brittany experience a mild temperate climate. Summers are slightly more reliable and warm and than those in Britain and temperatures can reach the 80s during peak season in July and August.

The shoulder seasons of spring and autumn are mild and see higher rainfall. Fortunately, rainy spells are fairly short lived and often interspersed with pleasant blue sky days.

Winter in this part of France is also less harsh than the UK, with severe frosts and sub zero temperatures a rare occurrence. November to

January are the wettest months however there is still a reasonable amount of winter sunshine.

When to Go?

Summer

During the summer season, you can do a multitude of everyday activities. In August, you won't have to wonder what to do on Thursdays. "Renc'arts" is an artistic event that takes place on Thursday evenings. These are free street performances that entertain the citizens of Saint-Malo as well as the vacationers.

You can also attend the festival that shakes up the town, the route du Rock.

Every year, the seaside resort also hosts the World Folklore Festival to pay homage to cultures from all corners of the globe and to give you a tour of the world without paying a fortune.

You can also attend some crewed racing like the Transat Québec Saint-Malo that takes place once every four years. On this occasion, you'll experience the excitement of the winners and enjoy the festive atmosphere that takes over the town.

Autumn

In autumn, the city is no longer "invaded" by tourists in love with Brittany. It is brought to life by boating enthusiasts that attend or participate in the famous race named the Route du Rhum. The competitors cast off from Saint-Malo to reach Guadeloupe a few days later, after having crossed the Atlantic Ocean. On this occasion, a village is built in the city and activities are offered to the crowds.

Winter

Why not adventure in Saint-Malo in Winter ?

Surely, swimming would be complicated and there are fewer activities than in Summer, but the temperatures are a lot milder than in the Alps. An added bonus: you can even listen to great music thanks to the winter version of the Route du Rock festival that takes place in February simultaneously in Rennes and Saint-Malo.

Obviously, you can also explore the beautiful city in Spring, before the crowds, and enjoy the mild temperatures due to its oceanic climate.

St-Malo Surrounding Area

While most visitors to St-Malo head to the citadel with its surrounding beaches and islands, there are additional places of interest in the immediate vicinity of the town (some within walking distance) that can sometimes get overlooked.

For those holidaying in the city during the peak season months of July and August, these provide an opportunity to venture further afield and escape from the summer crowds.

The Rance estuary and the English Channel lie on the immediate western and northern sides of St-Malo respectively, with the nearby suburbs of St-Servan and Parame to the south and west of the citadel.

Hotels in St-Malo

While some hotels inside the city walls are up to snuff, others are a bit run down. An alternative is to stay along the Plage du Sillon and walk the 10 min. into the historic center.

Hotel Alba

17 rue des Dunes

Phone 02-99-40-37-18

Facing the shimmering sea, this is the perfect beach-based hotel in St-Malo. You almost have the impression of staying on a boat, due to its proximity to the water; the smallish rooms gain in size thanks to their expansive views. Each is tastefully decorated in earthy tones, with modern, comfortable furnishings. The best rooms feature balconies and you can also choose from several family rooms. If you're not strolling on the beach at sunset, enjoy a drink on its terrace or its scenic bar.

Hotel Beaufort

25 Chaussee du Sillon, St-Malo, 35400, France

Phone 02-99-40-99-99

A neighbor to the Hotel Alba, recent renovations and new ownership have given this hotel modern amenities while retaining a seaside home feel. Rooms have spectacular beach and sunset views, and some rooms have a bed for a third person.

Breakfast for 13€ is served in a dining room looking out over the waves.

Hôtel France et Chateaubriand

12 pl. Chateaubriand

Phone 02-99-56-66-52

To experience the 19th-century heyday of the Emerald coast, there's no better place than at the birthplace of one of its heroes: writer Chateaubriand. Located inside the walls of old St-Malo, the flowering courtyard feels as though you've stepped into the Romantic era. Common areas still have this bygone feeling; however, guestrooms have been brought into the 21st century, the best and most modern rooms being the *chambres supérieures*. Request a room with views of the ramparts or the sea. Sip cool cocktails in the chic bar or dine in the regal restaurant with gold-trimmed Corinthian columns.

Quic en Grogne

8 rue d'Estrées

Phone 02-99-20-22-20

Ideally positioned on a quiet street close to shops and the beach, this is the perfect budget hotel intra-muros. The hotel finished a lengthy renovation in early 2014, giving it a fresh, contemporary feel. The small guestrooms have a subtle nautical theme while staying clear of kitsch. All bathrooms have been refitted; the more expensive ones have bathtubs. The best rooms look over a flowery courtyard. Breakfast is served in a glass-covered sunroom, and the hotel's convenient private parking allows guests to avoid the hassle of parking outside the ramparts.

Things to See in St-Malo

The 15th-century Porte St-Vincent, with a Belle Epoque carrousel just in front of it, is the main entrance to St-Malo *Intra-muros*. Walk to your right past the restaurant terraces on place Chateaubriand a portal leads to steps up to the ramparts. Built and rebuilt over several centuries, some parts of these walls date from the 14th century. Weather cooperating, they're an ideal place to start a walking tour and take in sweeping views of the English Channel and the Fort National.

About halfway round, you'll see an islet called the Ile du Grand-Bé during low tide you can walk to it and visit French Romantic novelist Chateaubriand's tomb. His last wish was to be buried here, where he'd "hear only the sounds of the wind and the ocean." Also within sight is the Piscine de Bon-Secours, a 1930s outdoor swimming pool whose three walls catch receding seawater. On warm days you'll see brave divers leaping from its cement platform.

If it's too windy, get off the ramparts by descending the ramp that joins rue de la Crosse. Turn left onto rue de la Pie Qui Boit and follow it until you reach rue Broussais. Alternatively, continue along the ramparts (where the view just keeps getting better) until you reach the Porte de Dinan. The street below it, rue de Dinan, becomes rue Broussais. Both routes lead to the place de Pilori back in the center. Head back toward the Porte St-Vincent for the greatest concentration of shopping and dining options.

Cathédrale St-Vincent

12 rue St-Benoît

Phone 02-99-40-82-31

Transformation of a monastic church into this cathedral began in 1146. Over the centuries, various architects added Romanesque, Gothic, and Neoclassical elements—only to have the steeple knocked off and the transept destroyed during fierce fighting in 1944. It took nearly 30 years to restore the structure and its magnificent stained glass. A floor mosaic commemorates the 1535 blessing of St-Malo native Jacques Cartier before he set off to discover Canada. Cartier's tomb is here, along with that of René Duguay-Trouin, a legendary privateer so successful he was made a commander in the French navy.

Fort National

Grande Plage de Sillon

Phone 06-72-46-66-26

Once you have loaded your car up with all of the holiday gear you need, you can recuperate on your crossing to the ancient city of St. Malo. Arriving at the wonderful old port as travellers have done over hundreds of years, it is easy to see why St. Malo is still popular today. As an important coastal town many of the tourist attractions are based around its pirate history and the sea.

The popular Fort National was constructed in 1689 on the orders of King Louis XIV to protect the port of St. Malo. Though it may not have the most in facilities, it definitely has wow factor. You will enjoy the guided tours, but the best feature is its location and the far reaching views that you can enjoy from its ramparts across the bay and the old town.

Musée d'Histoire de St-Malo

Porte St-Vincent

Phone 02-99-40-71-57

This museum is perfect for understanding the history and commercial importance of St-Malo. The buildings themselves, the keep and gatehouse of the Château de St-Malo, add to the experience. Exhibits use artifacts, ship models, and imagery to tell the stories of the city's most famous citizens Chateaubriand, Jacques Cartier, and the privateers Duguay-Trouin and Surcouf. A section is reserved for photos of the extensive damage the city incurred during World War II.

Restaurants in St-Malo

Satisfy your summer taste buds with the best ice cream in St-Malo at Sanchez, 9 rue Vieille Boucherie; tel. 02-99-56-67-17). With over 120 flavors, it'll be hard to choose, but we love their signature flavor "Le péché Malouin."

For a formal meal has one of the finest dining rooms in town.

Lunch on the half-shell

If you're driving east from St-Malo to Mont-St-Michel, consider a stop in Cancale—a harbor town famous for its oysters since the 17th century, when Louis XIV had them delivered regularly to Versailles.

Head to the northernmost end of the Port de la Houle, just beyond the jetty, where you'll see a handful of blue and white covered stalls selling shellfish out of crates. Come armed with a baguette and half-bottle of muscadet (easily found on the port's main street) and order a dozen oysters to go. The sellers will shuck them immediately and hand them to you on a plastic plate. Find a spot on a bench or the rocks, slurp down your mollusks and toss the shells onto the sun-bleached pile below.

For a second course, pop in to the Crêperie du port, 1 pl. du Calvaire, 7 quai Thomas (tel. 02-99-

89-60-66), for inventive buckwheat galettes and dessert crepes.

La Brasserie du Sillon

3 Chaussée du Sillon

Phone 02-99-56-10-74

Outside the city walls you'll find St-Malo's most innovative restaurant. Set in a lovely stone building facing the Sillon beach, the interior is refined and the best tables overlook the sea. Dishes are beautifully presented, though on the pricey side *à la carte,* savings can be made with their great value fixed-priced menus. Savor specialties such as fisherman's *choucroute,* scallops in butter sauce or filet mignon of pork with chestnuts, or you might be easily tempted by 13 different *plateaux de fruit de mer,* overflowing with freshly caught shrimp, periwinkle, crab and lobster.

Le Chalut

8 rue de la Corne-de-Cerf

Phone 02-99-56-71-58

French for "fish-net," here's where you can reel in the freshest catches in town. The kitschy nautical decor keeps this 1-Michelin-starred pearl well hidden. Some of Chef Jean-Philippe Foucat's creations include red mullet filets with marinated capers and artichokes drizzled with orange oil, John Dory with asparagus and fresh coriander, scallops with ginger and celery mousse or turbot with regional white Paimpol beans and lobster cream. Save a little room for the Chivas whiskey soufflé with citrus and passion fruit caramel. Reservations required.

Nightlife in St-Malo

For an evening of gambling, head to Le Casino Barrière, 2 chaussée du Sillon (www.casinosbarriere.com/en/saint-malo.html; tel. 02-99-40-64-00). You can also order dinner, sometimes accompanied by live music. You must present your passport.

For dancing, consider L'Escalier, La Buzardière (www.escalier.fr; tel. 02-99-81-65-56), open Thursday to Saturday midnight to 7am. The cover doesn't exceed 14€. You'll need wheels, as the club is in the countryside 5km (3 miles) east of town. It does have a free shuttle, however; for information and reservations call 06-85-31-27-64. Le 109, 3 rue des Cordiers (www.le-109.com; tel. 02-99-56-81-09), is a futuristic bar and dance club in a 300-plus-year-old vaulted cellar. It isn't as fashionable as L'Escalier, but is accessible without a car. It's open Tuesday to Sunday 8pm to 3am; the price of your first drink (10€–12€) is considered the cover charge.

Popular pubs include L'Aviso, 12 rue du Point du Jour (www.facebook.com/BarLAVISO; tel. 07-68-15-01-07), offering 300 types of beer and Breton beer on tap, and Pub Saint Patrick, 24 rue Sainte-Barbe ([tel] 02-99-56-66-90), serving 50 different Irish whiskeys, along with Breton beer. Concerts are regularly scheduled at the latter

Shopping in St-Malo

If you're in St-Malo on Tuesday or Friday between 8am and 1pm and want to experience a great Breton market, head for the Halle au Blé, in the heart of the old city. You can't miss the bustle and the hawking of seafood, fresh produce, local dairy products, and baked goods.

Check out Marin-Marine, 5 Grand Rue (tel. 02-99-40-90-32), for men's and women's fashions including mariner's shirts and Breton wool sweaters. Gauthier Marines, 2 rue Porcon de la

Barbinais (www.gauthiermarines.com; tel. 02-99-40-91-81), is a walk-in treasure chest of model ships, wooden sculpture, and marine-themed gift items.

Brittany's most revered chef and modern-day spice hunter, Olivier Roellinger, has an eponymous shop at 12 rue Saint-Vincent (www.epices-roellinger.com; [tel] 06-18-80-44-10). His beautifully presented blends, made from spices found all over the world, are worth collecting. And just try leaving Maison Larnicol, 6 rue St Saint-Vincent (www.chocolaterielarnicol.fr; tel. 02-99-40-57-62), empty handed. It specializes in Breton sweets including baked goods, chocolates, and a variety of flavored caramels.

1 Day experience in Malo

Saint Malo is 420 km's outside of Paris and about a 4 hour drive. Driving times will vary if you take the fast toll highways but be warned, for a short stretch of tolled highway, we paid €115! That's right! France's toll roads are notoriously expensive but there's apparently a new breed of private toll roads that are outrageously expensive but nonetheless liked by the smartphone's GPS.

It will be extremely difficult to find parking inside the walls of the old city. If you don't want to take the chance of meandering around the narrow alleys in search of parking, park the car outside the walls and do some walking.

As opposed to your car, you actually want to stay inside the old city walls if you'll be spending the night. There are plenty of small hotels and even more B&B's.

Saint Malo is famous for the forts scattered on tiny island in its bay. Some of these island forts are accessible by foot but only at low tide so check the tide schedule for Saint Malo and plan ahead.

The weather in this part of France can quickly change. In any case, it will be warm in the sun and chilly in the dark so it's best to dress in layers.

One of the perks of northern France is long days, starting in spring. The sun will fully set at only about 10pm in May so there's plenty of time for daytime sightseeing.

Getting There

We are arrived to Saint Malo at about noon on a busy Saturday. The weather along the drive from Paris was overcast and the forecast was for a cloudy day. As we got closer to Saint Malo, the sky cleared up and once again, the French weatherman was wrong! It was beginning to look like a beautiful spring day.

Our prebooked Airbnb was in an awesome location, right inside the city walls so despite the warnings, we decided to try our luck with parking the car inside the old city. I must admit that we simply got lucky. In one of the few tiny parking lots, we met a nice local woman who offered to move her car from the lot and into her private parking spot a few blocks from there. If it wasn't for this lucky break, we would have been screwed.

The Beach & Forts

After settling in our basic accommodation, we headed out to explore the town. A natural starting point for us was the northern beach, home to two special islands: the Petit Bé & Grand

Bé. After passing by the pétanque players, we descended down to the golden beach.

The Petit Bé & Grand Bé are small islands just off the coast. The Petit Bé is home to an old fort that was used by the French army to defend the strategic port of Saint Malo until 1885. The Grand Bé is, as its name suggest, the bigger of the two and is accessible by foot from the mainland at low tide. The famous French writer and local hero François-René de Chateaubriand is buried on the Grand Bé and making the hike up to Chateaubriand's tomb is a popular thing to do in Saint Malo.

Though we did have incredible luck with the weather, this wasn't the case with the tide, which really calls the shots around here. We arrived just when the tide was starting to roll back, covering the footpath leading up to the

Grand Bé. A bit disappointed, the view from the beach is still worth the visit! The sand is golden and the air fresh with the smell of the sea.

The next natural thing to do was to join the onlookers on the city walls and walk along to get a view of the Fort National. As yet another fort to protect the strategic port, the Fort National was built in 1689 and was actually occupied by Nazi Germany during WWII. This area of France was strategic to Hitler and the fort was part of the Atlantic Wall fortification plan. When the allies bombed Saint Malo, the fort was used as a prison until liberation in 1944.

Today, the Fort National is open to the public and is accessible only at low tide in certain parts of the year. Check out the visitors information page for opening times and rates.

Exploring the Old Walled City

Heading back inside the city walls, it was finally time to explore the old city. If you think Saint Malo is cute on the outside, it's even cuter on the inside. Narrow medieval lanes are filled with local delights and cute little spots. Being on the coast, seafood is very popular here as you would expect but since we are in Brittany, the true rulers of the streets are the creperies! The French love this wonder from Brittany and pretty much anything goes as a filling, from cheese to bacon you name it.

While Isabelle and her mother did some shopping, I headed over to explore the local cathedral, Cathédrale Saint-Vincent-de-Saragosse de Saint-Malo, or more commonly known the Saint-Malo Cathedral. If you've read some of my posts, you know that I'm a sucker for old European churches. I'm always amazed at the amount of work that was put into these places of worship centuries ago (whether rightfully so or not...). The local cathedral is nothing special aside from the beautiful stained glass windows, which I've found to radiate a blend of colors that I have yet to see in other cathedrals. Maybe it was the angle of the sun or maybe not, it's worth the visit just to see these windows.

Back on the streets, I found my two ladies queueing up at the famous local bakery –les Délices du Gouverneur. If you visit Saint Malo there's really one thing you need to taste, aside from crepes, and that is a *kouign-amann*. Definitely not for calorie counters, this Breton cake consists of layers of dough, butter and sugar giving meaning to name kouign-amann (butter bread). I can't say it's my favorite pastry of all time but you gotta taste it if you've made the trip.

All that butter bread will make you thirsty and there's no better place to grab a drink than in the sunny terrace of Charly's Bar. On a day like this, I recommend jazzing up your beer. We went for a *monaco* (beer with grenadine) and a *demi peche* (shandy) the perfect drink at the perfect time!

Walking Along the Ramparts

At this point, the sun was shining in full force so it was a good idea to step out from the shadows of old city and walk along the Saint Malo ramparts. Just head in the direction of the wall and you'll find steps to lead you up above town. The view on a sunny day is gorgeous! You'll be treated to panoramic views of the beautiful coast.

A good deviation before heading back inside the walls is to walk along the coast towards the lighthouse. On a sunny day like this, locals folks are out and about, playing a social round of pétanque, doing some fishing or simply baking in the sun.

Tough Choices for Dinner

Not really wanting this day to end, we headed back along the walls and settled in the tiny terrace of Le Corps de Garde. This creperie has fine seaside views but we came here for a pre dinner round of cider, another local delight from Brittany. With only 2.5% alcohol, you really need to be careful not to chug this down too quickly or maybe you should.

The view from this spot is amazing, with the sun beginning to drop right in front of you. We wanted to wait for the sunset but the days are starting to get so long and our stomachs made the tough call to get moving.

For dinner, you have plenty of options in the center of the old town but for the best selection of places to have dinner in Saint Malo, head over to Rue Jacques Cartier. Restaurant after restaurant will lure you in with their seafood & crepe specials. They don't even make the choice of 'and/or' hard why not just have both some seafood *and* a crepe? The best deals are for mussels & fries (moule frites) and a side crepe for only €10. Be warned though that the closer you get to the Hotel de Ville, the more touristy the restaurants begin to be.

The Most Amazing Sunset

We finished dinner at about 10pm and there was still a bit of light outside. The walk back to the B&B took us through the quiet streets of Saint Malo, beautifully lit up at night yet still dark enough to create a special atmosphere.

With the last rays of light still visible, I felt the urge to head back to the spot where we had the pre dinner cider and my hunch was right. As the sun was heading west, the same place where we started our visit a few hours ago was now illuminated by the deep red colors of the setting sun. Above the Petit & Grand Bé, you could see Venus & Jupiter making an appearance in the night sky what a great way to end our one day in Saint Malo adventure!

Closing Thoughts

Isabelle was totally right in insisting we make the trip to Saint Malo! It was actually a no brainer in retrospect. Though the climax was planned for the following day's visit to Mont Saint Michel, our one day in Saint Malo was super unique. While you are only a few hours away from Paris, you really feel the difference in Brittany and

Saint Malo is a real gem. There were a few things here and there that we missed and if you spend a few days in Brittany, this could be good place to base yourself in. Overall, in one day, we got a good taste of the area and the great weather certainly made the difference!

2 Days Experience in St. Malo

Touch down

Sail to St-Malo as a foot passenger on Brittany Ferries (0871 244 1400) from Portsmouth, or Condor Ferries (0845 609 1024) from Weymouth or Poole (with a Channel Islands stop) to St-Malo. Ferries dock at the international ferry terminal (2), a 10-minute walk from the city centre.

Ryanair (0871 246 0000) flies to Dinard from East Midlands and London Stansted. There is no public transport from the airport to St-Malo, so book a taxi before leaving the UK with Taxis-

Malouins (0033 2 99 81 30 30). Expect a fare of about €30.

For train travel, take a Eurostar (08705 186 186) from London St Pancras to Paris Gare du Nord, then Metro Line 4 to Paris Montparnasse and the TGV to St-Malo. The journey should take about six hours. Return fares start at £135.

Get your bearings

Almost everything good about St-Malo is concentrated in the part of the city within the old walls la citadelle. Construction of the walls began in the Middle Ages and continued until the end of the 17th century, with further expansion between 1708 and 1744. Sadly, the original walls were all-but-destroyed by bombing in 1944 and had to be rebuilt, although a section dating from 1145 remains on the west side of the citadelle.

The Cathedral St-Vincent (3), on Place Jean de Chatillon, dominates the skyline. The 15-century castle (4), housing the municipal museum, is in the citadelle's south-east corner. Beyond the walls lie an attractive harbour, islets, forts and spectacular beaches to explore.

The tourist office (5) is just outside the city walls on Esplanade Saint-Vincent (00 33 2 99 56 64 43). Open 9am-1pm and 2pm-6.30pm daily except Sundays, when it opens 10am-12.30pm and 2.30pm-6pm; there are longer hours in July and August.

Check in

If you want to stay within the walls, expect to pay a premium. Hôtel de l'Univers (00 33 2 99 40 89 52) is on Place Chateaubriand (6). Doubles from €116 in high season; breakfast is €9 per person.

Hôtel Elizabeth (7) at 2 Rue des Cordiers (00 33 2 99 56 24 98) occupies one of the rare 16th-century buildings that survived the Second World War. Doubles from €105 including breakfast.

A couple of kilometres beyond the city walls is the Grand Hôtel des Thermes (8) on the Grande Plage (00 33 2 99 40 75 00), with fantastic views and a health spa. A double room costs €184 in high season; breakfast is €21 per person.

Day one

Window shopping

The cobbled streets within the old walls are a shopper's delight. Hours can be whiled away browsing the boutiques and craft shops. High on the list for book lovers should be Librairie Septentrion (9) at 2 Place Brevet, a specialist in old tomes and antique texts.

St-Malo also has more than 20 galleries dotted around its narrow streets, ranging from specialists in contemporary ceramics and jewellery to traditional landscape and maritime art. To help point you in the right direction, pick up a guide to the city's offerings from the tourist office.

Lunch on the run

For a quick lunch head to the Lion d'Or (00 33 2 99 56 36 02) on Place Chateaubriand (6). Grab a table in the sun and order the Marmite de St-Jacques a leek, mushroom and scallop stew, served in a pot with rice. Not cheap at €16 but simply divine.

Take a hike

A walk along the ramparts that guard the old city is a pure joy. Start with a visit to the castle and the city museum (4), open 10am to noon and

2pm to 6pm daily from April to September; €5.40. Exhibitions chart the city's prosperity, taking visitors through the ages, from the intrepid explorer Jacques Cartier, coloniser of Canada, and François-René de Chateaubriand, the trailblazer of romanticism in French literature, through to the Second World War and the devastation and subsequent reconstruction of the old city.

Exit the museum and make your way anti-clockwise around the ramparts taking note of the Fort National, across the bay, built during the reign of King Louis XIV in 1689.

Continue anti-clockwise, passing the Tour Bidouane lookout (10) over Grand Bé island, the burial place of Chateaubriand. At low tide it can be reached on foot using a cobbled path. Should you choose to visit, be sure to keep one eye on the tide because the path can become quickly submerged. Alternatively, choose to remain at your vantage point on the ramparts, where fun can be had watching a small flotilla of boats assemble, ready to help any stranded tourists as the tide rolls in. Carry on to the Bastion de la Hollande (11) where a statue of Jacques Cartier takes in the view over the Rance river estuary. Stop and gaze out over the river to the town of Dinard and Cap Fréhel beyond.

Make your way round towards the Great Gate (12), the oldest in St-Malo. Be sure to take in the view down the Grand Rue towards the Cathedral St Vincent (3). Complete your walk by continuing on to the St Vincent Gate, the exterior of which is decorated with the coat of arms of Brittany, pausing to peer down on the busy Place Chateaubriand (6), before rejoining the bustle of the citadelle.

An apéritif

For something a bit different try Café La Java (13) at 3 Rue Sainte-Barbe (00 33 2 99 56 41 90). It is owned by Jean-Jacques Samoy, who invites you to "enter my madness". Swings greet you at the bar and the café is adorned with memorabilia including kitsch postcards and antique instruments. Order a Kir Breton for €3, a delicious local concoction combining cassis and cider, and let your eyes wander over the weird and wonderful.

Dining with the locals

The restaurant Bouche en Folie (14) at 14 Rue du Boyer (00 33 6 72 49 08 89) is a delightful little place offering two courses at €22, three for €28. Menus change every couple of weeks or so; the cooking is first rate. If available a meal of terrine of rabbit, followed by sea bream and creamy risotto and finishing with a selection of local cheeses, is particularly recommended.

Day two

Sunday morning: go to church

Construction of the Cathedral St Vincent (3) began the 1100s but its distinctive spire was not added until the 19th century. The original nave was enlarged in the 1500s and underwent many changes and renovations in the 18th and 19th centuries. Today it boasts a spectacular rose window, designed in 1968 by Raymond Cornon. Mass is held every Sunday at 10am, 11.30am and 6pm.

A walk on the beach

The Plage du Sillon (15) is a sweep of golden sands running east from the citadelle. Strike out for the Pointe de Rochebonne 3km away, taking care over a particularly seaweedy stretch just over half-way. If you are feeling energetic, continue on to Rothéneuf and take the chance to visit the Rochers Sculptés (00 33 2 99 56 23 95), a series of monsters and dragons carved into the rocks by a hermit, Father Adolphe Fouré, in the 1870s. They are open daily between April and October, from 9am-7pm (longer hours in July and August but not in bad weather). Admission €2.50. It's a good 6km walk back so if your legs are a little weary head into central Rothéneuf and catch a bus back to St-Malo. Route No 3 gets you to the railway station for €1.05.

Out to brunch

Brunch in St-Malo means only one thing: a galette washed down with a cup of local cider no it's never too early. Try the Crêperie Le Tournesol (16) at 4 Rue des Marins (00 33 2 99 40 36 23), with its terrace spilling out on to cobbled streets, from 11.30am Sunday. Its speciality galettes start at €5.50 and come with a huge variety of fillings, from smoked Breton sausage and egg to goats' cheese and Camembert. If you still have room, finish with something sweet a crêpe with hot chocolate sauce is €3.50.

Take a view

For a great view of the citadelle in all its glory, exit the intra-muros at the Dinan Gate (17) and turn right. Head out along the 500m-long pier, enjoying views over the outer harbour to Saint-Servan, before turning to take in the panorama of the walls and the skyline of the old town.

Cultural afternoon

The House of Poets and Writers (18) at 5 Rue du Pélicot (00 33 2 99 40 28 77) dates back to 1676 and is one of only a handful of wood-fronted houses left in the citadelle. Today it hosts exhibitions, conferences and workshops ranging from literary walks to poetry translations. Recent exhibitions have included "Rougerie éditions: 60 ans et plus de résistance en poésie", marking 62 years of René Rougerie's poetry reviews, and "Labyrinthes", engravings and paintings by René Le Hérissé.

Icing on the cake

For a different perspective on the city take a sea-bus from the Cale de Dinan (19) over to the town of Dinard. The journey takes a mere 10 minutes (€6.70 return) but offers great views back over to St-Malo and down the River Rance.

St Malo beaches

A charming walled Old City, a string of golden sand beaches and a dramatic natural setting combine to make St Malo one of Brittany's premier tourist resorts. Constructed on a granite rock jutting out of the English Channel (La

Manche) the Old City of St Malo, encircled protectively by 6m (20ft) thick walls, is the resort's principal attraction. During the summer months its narrow streets come alive as a throng of holidaymakers descend to take in the views from the ramparts or admire the centrepiece St Vincent Cathedral. Along the coast St Servan, Parme and Rotheneuf also form part of the St Malo resort. Here golden beaches, a variety of watersports, which run the gamut from sea kayaking to windsurfing, and a phalanx of resort hotels cater to the tourists' every need.

Beach:

The St Malo beach resort boasts a number of golden sand beaches, with the most popular trio located just outside the Old City. The sheltered Mole is favoured by sun worshippers and at the height of summer it can be difficult for holidaymakers to find a stretch of sand on which to unfurl their towels. Bon Secours with its large saltwater pool and sailing club is also a good bet. Sillon is another popular spot for wind-powered watersports.

Beyond the beach:

Holidaymakers gain a different perspective of the Old City as they walk around the 2km (1.5-mile) stretch of 14th-century granite ramparts (accessed from Porte St Vincent). From there they can look out over Saint Malo's rooftops and soak up panoramic views of the bay and its islets, before exploring the maze of medieval streets and admiring the vault of St Vincent Cathedral.

Family fun:

Justifiably popular with families, St Malo entertains children with its sandy beaches, a smorgasbord of watersports and resort hotels that typically boast swimming pools and kids clubs. Kids and adults alike will be thrilled by the sharks and turtles at the Grand Aquarium (Avenue du General Patton).

Exploring further:

A rocky islet dominated by an imposing Benedictine abbey (constructed between the 11th and 16th centuries), the historic settlement of Mont Saint-Michel, a UNESCO World Heritage site, is an impressive sight. This important European pilgrimage spot can be reached in just over an hour by bus from St Malo and is well worth a visit for the photo opportunities alone.

(Boat trips) >>: When the tide is in, the inshore forts are among the destinations of the popular boat trips that operate out of Saint Malo.There is a wide choice of pleasure cruise options, including mini-cruises around Saint Malo, longer cruises along the coast, or simply a trip across the mouth of the Rance to the resort of Dinard on the other side. There are also excursions up the river via the unique Rance tidal power dam, and beyond to the picturesque small town of Dinan.

The (Etoile du Roy) >>. Fora more historic experience, one of Saint Malo's other big attractions ... as long as it is in port.. is the *Etoile du Roy,* the second largest replica tall ship in France. For most of the year, she is moored in the port, close to the tourist office. The Etoile was originally built as the *Grand Turk* for the British ITV series *Hornblower*, and has appeared in several films and TV series.

(Tour Solidor) >>. A little bit further from the historic centre is the Tour Solidor, a fine 14th century keep that now houses the Museum of Saint Malo and its area.

Things to Do in St-Malo

Get a ferry over to St Malo

With slight fear in our bellies, we boarded our Brittany Ferry on a Friday night and said a prayer for calm seas. After our experience abandoning ship in Croatia, we were slightly apprehensive about spending a solid 12 hours aboard a boat without knowing how the sea conditions were going to be treating us. And we couldn't exactly jump off like in Croatia, unless we fancied swimming to Guernsey.

Brittany Ferries is a great way to travel over to France, especially if you want to take your car over for a road-trip. They operate out of three UK ports, including Portsmouth (the closest port to Bristol), and sail to seven destinations in Spain and France. There are a variety of different cabins you can book and they all come at different rates according to the cabin standard we had a twin room with just enough room to swing a cat and a porthole to view the expansive ocean swallowing up the distant cliffs of England.

With a bit of shopping on board, a cinema, a few bars and cafes, and a fancy restaurant (I call it fancy as there was an old man playing a piano for the diners. Fancy.), you have more than enough to entertain yourself in the evening. Before you know it, the prosseco is gone and your belly is fully of delicious roast salmon. To bed, and with any luck, wake up in St-Malo!

Rich Maritime History

The castle of Saint-Malo, east of the town, was built by the Dukes of Brittany and later sold to the king of France. It has since been restored, damaged, restored and further damaged right up until the liberation of St. Malo during WWII. There are plenty of displays to see including maritime artifacts, but the best part of the visit for many is the view from the tower.

St. Malo is also famous for being the location of the world's first tidal power station. This attracts around 200,000 visitors each year who are interested in viewing the lock in the west end of a dam which allows the passage of 16,000 vessels between the English Channel and the Rance.

Saint-Malo Cathedral

Another wonderful place to go in St. Malo is the Catholic cathedral of Saint-Vincent-de-Saragosse de Saint-Malo. The cathedral is a national monument of France and formerly the seat of the Bishop of Saint-Malo. Many visitors point out that is not dissimilar to Notre Dame in Paris. The best time to visit is early in the day when the light streams through the lovely stained glass window and the whole building does tend to become a little dark later in the day.

St. Malo can be a great place to visit if you are on a short trip to France, but it is also somewhere that you can leave behind as you move on to other interesting areas of Brittany, a region that enjoys sunny weather warmed by the Gulf Stream and the occasional windy season, enjoyed by wind surfers from around the world.

Explore before the crowds appear

With a distinctively creepy wake-up call of Brittany music playing over the loudspeakers, we got showered and changed in our en-suite rooms before we dropped anchor. Really well rested and fresh, we docked and walked the brief 20 minutes to the gates of St-Malo.

On arrival, flat, white skies washed out the light and gave a slightly eerie aura as we entered the citadel. Little did we realise that it was such a ghost town because it was ridiculously early in the morning, but now on reflection, we're real glad we got to see the city before everyone finally hauled themselves out of bed to clutter the streets.

Past a silent old-fashioned carousel, we entered into St-Malo and trotted over cobblestones to a café for our caffeine injection. Friendly waiters welcomed us with flourish at Café de Louest and we slowly woke up along with the residents. I was physically restrained from charging into the quaintest bakery for a fresh pastry as we were about to embark on a foodie tour of St-Malo.

Take a short Foodie Tour of St-Malo

Hey, we all love food and so a foodie tour shouldn't be too hard to get excited about. But did you know that St-Malo is famed for its salted caramel? Its salted fresh butter? Its harvested scallops? And that there's such a thing as butter cake?? Hopefully you're drooling already as it was all as good as it sounds.

We met Corrine, a Brit who had escaped to this seaside town, who took us around the quaint cobbled streets, winding us between the houses to hidden nooks and crannies where we discovered St-Malo's foodie scene.

A top thing to do in St-Malo is to see fresh Kouign Amnn being made. We saw some being rolled by an exceptional French baker who was actually wearing a striped top (we appreciated the authenticity) and got to sample the fresh cake straight from the oven. I also got to taste the famous Bordier butter that is championed by chefs all around France, especially in Paris, and got a pot of salted butter caramel which I have had to hide so I don't eat it straight out the jar.

As well as dining on all the treats, we got to know a bit of St-Malo's history. In the 14th Century, it claimed itself to be an independent republic shaking off connections with the rest of France and charged any English ships passing up the Channel. Foreign ships were pillaged by St-Malo's corsairs (official pirates) in the 17th/18th century, which made the city's sailor merchants incredibly wealthy. So basically, St-Malo was were the French pirates used to hang out back in the day not such a quaint seaside town now?

Pick up some stripes or a fisherman rain mac

As small St-Malo seems a large volume of tourists, from both England and Paris, the retail industry is booming. Shops line the streets and have many a Breton strip top or adorable fisherman raincoat hung out the front.

Pick up some pick n mix at the sweet shops, peruse the ceramic bowls, indulge in some glorious ice cream and pop into the quirky shops. You can while away a few hours browsing the stores in the walls of la citadelle, and don't forget to pop your head into the spice shop; an apothecary of spices stacked up on sky-high shelves. If you want to explore 12 different kinds of vanilla, then this is the place to do it.

Eat your body weight in crêpes

A visit to St-Malo shouldn't be without a taste of famous breton galette, aka crêpes. These savoury crêpes are made from blé noir buckwheat flour meaning hungry gluten-free visitors do not have a thing to worry about. They're light and crispy, and although they look thin they sure pack a punch and are a filling meal.Try a Breton crêpe with cheese, egg and veggies for a brunch that really hits the spot.

We were served the traditional ice cold cider with our pancakes at Le Crops de Garde, and finished off our feasting with a sweet crêpe. Ice cream, cream, chocolate sauce decadent but impossible to say no!

Champagne at Café La Java

When you want to sip down a sophisticated beverage in a famous setting, be sure to head to St-Malo's quirky cafe, Café la Java.

Order a freshly popped glass of champagne at this eccentric bolthole of puppets and dolls. Vintage posters cover what little space you can see of the walls, and thousands of figures stare resolutely down at you. Slightly off-putting, but distract yourself by perching on a swing at the bar or in a wrought iron bench for two.

Scoot around on segways

Now I've never tried a segway before and i was quite apprehensive about getting on one mainly for the 'cool' factor. I'd seen so many on trips away and scoffed at them, but I ate my words once I got to grips with my trusty two-wheeled steed.

Tilt forwards to go, tilt back to slow, push the handlebars to the left to turn left and push them right to turn (you guessed it) right you can soon pick up a good amount of speed and zip past any judging eyes! Alex was beyond stoked to ride one as she can't ride a bike and was worried it would be a failed mission. Thankfully she couldn't keep her segway once the trip was over

For 1.5 hours, you can grab a group of friends and take off on your seaways to far-flung corners of the citadel. Touring by segway is a top thing to do in St-Malo, and it was actually really useful as we got to head up to the hilltop park really fast. We got panoramic views of the bay below and Plage du Sillon France's third most beautiful beach all in a speedy rev of our segways. If you have more time, heading up the the park and along the beach would make for a brilliant walk it would certainly walk off a few crêpes!

Dine over the rooftops of St-Malo at Le 5 Restaurant

When the sun begins to set and hunger strikes, you must head to a restaurant which will serve only the best seafood. As St-Malo's industry (prior to tourism) was dominated by fishing, they've had centuries to perfect their seafood dishes and sculpt delicious flavours into their fish menus.

We headed up to the top floor of Le Chateaubriand Hotel to a small restaurant, Restaurant Le 5, that overlooks the rooftops of St-Malo and the sea beyond the fort walls.

Dine on a real fishy fruit de mer (seafood) where it is authentically served pretty fresh from the sea. It was definitely an eye-opening experience as I've never had to get to grips with so much shell and really get stuck in at extracting tasty morsels a pretty intense starter, but hey, I tried snails for my first time!

The main was an exquisite fish dish with fragrant foam, matched with a 2014 Menetou-Salon, and it was followed by a myriad of teeny little desserts. A beautifully put together three course dinner.

Enjoy a cocktail in St-Malo's hidden city secrets Bar l'Alchimiste

I do enjoy a cocktail, in case you haven't noticed, and so when we found this cocktail bar down an alleyway nearly besides our hotel, we rejoiced. Delicious drinks AND we don't have to walk far to get home?? Sorted.

Bar l'Alchimiste is a dark and strange watering hole with pretty chairs outside on the grey cobbled alleyway. Outside, you can enjoy a tall glass of Kir Royale a refreshing French cocktail of crème de cassis topped with champagne and take in the fresh sea air. This bar gets busier in the evenings, but for an al fresco drink in the warm Breton air, head here for a brilliant cocktail.

Stay at Le Chateaubriand Hotel

We had the pleasure of staying at the central hotel, Le Chateaubriand Hotel. Tucked away off the main strip when you enter the walls of St-Malo, this tall hotel boasts a gorgeous entrance of flowers and cacti, and a conservatory of comfortable chairs and plush fabrics.

With 20 rooms facing the sea, we managed to snag a room with a view over the fort walls it felt brilliant to open those wide windows and get a fresh breeze coming straight off the sea.

St-Malo is a fantastic port town to jump start your trip in France. A weekend is all you need to fully explore all it's hidden secrets and sample the local cuisine and champers, but if you have a bit more time then the wider region is definitely worth an explore!

Grab your car, load up with road-trip supplies and catch the ferry down to St-Malo this summer get a cool-box and bring me back some of that darn good salty seaweed Bordier butter. Bread and butter never tasted as good as in St-Malo!

Saint-Malo Walls

The ramparts protect the entirety of the old part of Saint-Malo and from a circuit of 1.75 kilometres.

They were started in the 1100s, updated to combat new military technology in the 1600s and then expanded again up to the mid-18th century.

When you do the walk be sure to have some literature with you, because every gate, bastion and view has a story to tell.

Go up for panoramas of the sea, the Grand Bé island, Fort National, Dinard across the water and the magnificent granite homes of the city's wealthy ship-owners, and come down if you see a shop or crêperie that takes your fancy.

Grande'Porte on the eastern side is flanked by two chunky bastions and guards the narrow finger of land that links the walled city what are now Saint-Malo's suburbs.

Old Saint-Malo

With grey granite as the their material, Saint-Malo's houses have a distinguished air that borders on severe, but is always beautiful.

The "Intra-Muros" district is all cobblestone streets with bars, restaurants, upmarket shops and crêperies, and exploring is the name of the game.

The sense of the city's venerability is so strong that it almost seems impossible that most of

Saint-Malo needed to be restored after 1944. It's a difficult task to choose; the most picturesque are in old Saint-Malo, but Rue Jacques Cartier is gorgeous.

Here on the east side of the walled city the houses are built into the defences and the ground floor is one long string of cafes and restaurants.

Plage du Sillon

One of those dynamic beaches in a constant state of flux, Plage du Sillon is three kilometres of fine sand beginning just north of the walled city.

On the edge is a great embankment, built at the turn of the 20th century and spanning more than a kilometre and a half.

This makes for easy strolling at any time of year, to work up an appetite and see the kites at low tide.

On gentle summer days families come for the smooth sand and can bathe in the shallow rock pools on the western edge by Fort National.

Then on blustery winter days the sea will crash against the embankments at high tide.

Grand Aquarium Saint-Malo

A quick bus ride from the walled city will land you at Saint-Malo's aquarium, a high-profile day out that is updated almost every new season.

For those holidaying with little guys it's a rainy day attraction that also ties in neatly with the city's seafaring history.

You can't talk about the animals without mentioning the 360° shark aquarium, which was added in 2011 and holds 600,000 litres.

In another tank the wreck of a historic galleon is a home for white-tip and black -tip sharks.

Elsewhere the aquarium synthesises environments from around the world, so the mangrove has piranhas, four-eyed fish and turtles and the tropical tank has coral and colourful species like clownfish and surgeonfish

Paramé

The district next to Plage du Sillon, northeast of the walled city, grew quickly in the late 19th century furnishing it with many stunning Belle Époque villas.

These were built by wealthy holidaymakers, who gave free rein to their sense of whimsy.

With an itinerary you could have a little walking tour of this leafy neighbourhood, stopping to see fabulous houses like Villa l'Argonne on Boulevard Chateaubriand, which has a stunning octagonal tower and a pattern of alternating glazed and red bricks.

Then Villa Remember on Boulevard Hébert is in an exaggerated Flemish style, with a crow-stepped gable and stone finial.

Fort National

The engineering mastermind Vauban drew up plans for this forward bastion on the Îlette rock at the western end of Plage du Sillon.

It bears his tell-tale star configuration, and was the final piece in Saint-Malo's defensive puzzle, conceived to protect the city from the British navy.

It did just this job in 1693 when it helped to fend off an Anglo-Dutch attack.

Much later it became a makeshift prison for the German forces in the last days of their occupation in 1944. The fortress is open in the summer for tours, and is a perfect document of 17th-century military design.

You'll know when you come for a look around because the French tricolour will be flying.

Grand Bé

You also have to wait for low tide to access Grand Bé, another islet a few strides from the ramparts.

In the Second World War rocky little islands such as this became a useful spot location for German gun emplacements.

When the Americans liberated Saint-Malo Grand Bé fell quickly, but it was weeks before the Alet peninsula at the mouth of the Rance River would surrender.

Many come to Grand Bé to pay their respects to the romantic writer Chateaubriand, whose grave faces the sea as he had requested 20 years before he died.

GR-34

The Sentier des Douaniers (Custom's Officers' Trail) is exactly what it says it is: A coastal footpath devised in the 1700s to foil smugglers.

If you wanted you could start from Saint-Malo and walk all the way to Brest in Finistère.

But you may need to allow 25 days to walk these 400 kilometres, so it's not exactly a day trip! Instead you could pass a memorable day hiking the Côte d'Émeraude (Emerald Coast), on either side of Saint-Malo.

You'll encounter pale windswept beaches, granite cliffs, meadows flecked with wildflowers, oyster and mussel beds and many bunkers and pillboxes from the Second World War.

Parc de la Briantais

On high ground by the Rance Estuary is a sumptuous English park that once formed the grounds of the Château de la Briantais.

The estate belonged to rich ship-owners, who built a baroque mansion here in 1666, and the eerie but handsome ruins of this building are still visible in the park.

A newer château from the 19th century is still going strong as a cultural centre, with art exhibitions and concerts for jazz and classical music.

Visit for meditative walks on avenues dotted with sculptures, and to see those exhilarating views.

You can see Saint-Malo, Dinard and the entirety of the Rance Estuary.

Les Malouinières

Many people made large fortunes from privateering from the 16th to the 19th centuries, and in the vicinity of Saint-Malo are five lavish houses that the ship-owners left behind.

All are open to the public to different degrees in summer, and they're known as "Malouinières", which derives from the name of the city.

One of the most accessible is Puits Sauvage, which has been in the same family for more than 200 years.

On a self-guided tour you'll cross the dainty French parterre and see stables, dovecotes, oratory, bakery and a gigantic glass roof that measures 260 square metres and sustains a marvellous cactus garden.

Musée Jacques Cartier

The only surviving house belonging to the man who discovered Canada, the Manoir de Limoëlou was Cartier's summer residence in the years after he returned from his voyage.

The interior has been redecorated with period furniture and the various rooms now have the same function they would have filled when Cartier lived here.

Those new to his feats will get the lowdown here on a guided tour, during which you get to see some of the navigation instruments that Cartier used.

Tours are in French only, but there's an English guidebook and the museum's film also has an English language option.

Mémorial 39/45

As we mentioned, it took weeks for German resistance to be broken at Saint-Malo, and they dug in at this anti-aircraft bunker in the Cité d'Alet, set in the courtyard of a 17th-century fortress that had also been designed by Vauban.

Memorial 39/45 is an exhibition that recreates the war years in Saint-Malo, and is set in the vast bunker that measures more than 500 square metres, with three levels and ten rooms.

You'll be thrown into this dark chapter of the city's past with the help of authentic documents, weapons, uniforms and the specially-made historical film "The Battle of Saint-Malo".

Dinard

Across from Saint-Malo, on left bank of the Rance, Dinard has been given the epithet the "Nice of the North" for its stately atmosphere.

On the way you may be intrigued to know that the bridge that crosses the Rance estuary also houses Europe's first tidal power plant, built in 1966 and still working.

Once you get to Dinard you'll be dazzled by the luxurious mansions, from the late 19th century when the resort became "the" place to be seen in the summer season.

Many of these palatial homes are now listed and can be seen from the Promenade du Clair de Lune, which meanders along with coastline, has views of Saint-Malo and is beautifully lit on summer evenings.

Breton Cuisine

Seafood should be high on your culinary agenda in Saint-Malo.

Cancale, Brittany's oyster capital, is minutes east of the city.

Cancale's oyster fame goes back to Roman times when they were eaten by the Julius Caesar's legions, while Louis XIV had them expressly delivered from this town every day.

And it may be obvious, but the crêpe is almost synonymous with Brittany.

Have them sweet, or try the savoury alternative, galettes, which are made with buckwheat flour.

Another Breton speciality, cider is also big in Saint-Malo; it's sweet and acidic, with a light fizz and is the dream partner for galettes with ham and cheese.

The End

CPSIA information can be obtained
at www.ICGtesting.com
Printed in the USA
LVHW111121170722
723697LV00003B/212